Romanticized Confessions

Delbar Nonahal

Editing by Jane Freeborn and Delbar Nonahal

Cover and interior design by Nuno Moreira, NM DESIGN

ISBN Hardcover: 979-8-9853896-0-9

ISBN Paperback: 979-8-9853896-1-6

Romanticized Confessions

58 poems

Delbar Nonahal

A book of dedications

For all of you, but mainly, for myself.

TABLE OF CONTENTS

To the reader, an introduction.

I know I am supposed to hate myself, but I do not. I like the normalcy of my mud brown eyes, they fit perfectly alongside the mundane brown of my curtain-banged hair. The crook in my nose no longer bothers me as much as it once did. With reading glasses and a good angle I imagine it becomes barely visible. And while my body takes up quite a bit of space, it is the one I have. I aim not to bother myself too much with that, and not in the "bodies are temporary anyway" sense. Quite frankly, my body deserves to take up as much space as it would like to, for as long as it wants to. However, it is true that I have been conditioned to believe I am ugly my entire life. Fortunately for me, I had no clue.

Therefore, what stands before you today is an emerging adult who lacks the deep rooted self hatred that begins in early childhood. I was unaware of my fatness until about the age of nine when an older girl on the playground proclaimed it rather matter-of-factly. Sometimes I wonder which parent she overheard that from.

After that, I started to notice the little things: the struggle to find a bathing suit in the summer - the hesitation in my mother's eyes when I lept to do something physically challenging - the "your face is so beautiful" from relatives. Sometimes I wonder how much more I could have done, could have become, if I was not constantly limited by others because they believed I was incapable of accomplishing a task. The thing is, I am not ugly.

Every human being is beautiful because they are alive.

This is my story - the story of a girl who fell in love, quite a few times, and who happens to be fat. Not the story of a fat girl who miraculously found someone to love her. Let it serve as a reminder for those who feel unworthy of love and attraction that they are every bit as desirable as they may sit and wish to be.

One last note: I love cheesy. The result of having to learn in adolescence what it means to be loved from movies and books, rather than from another. I live for cheesy, and as a child I dreamt for it. Now an adult, I cling to cheesy whenever I can find it, and create it wherever I see the opportunity. I implore you to embrace the cheesy; to experience life in the gooiest way.

Love letters to myself, my foremost love.
And possibly to those who relate.

I do not mind normalcy, a consequence of spending my life constantly perceived by others as "inspiring" or "brave". I wanted to be normal. But it comes with the territory – living as a big girl while also holding no hesitations toward existing happily – it shocks people.

I am at my very core a big girl, and therefore no longer granted the privilege of normalcy. Even if I were to snap my fingers one morning and magically appear in the body I am sure others wish I had – others who would certainly find it much easier to love me then. Being fat is an intrinsic part of my nature. It is how I grew up. I am content in how I appear, although I pity those around me, constantly stuck in internal battles of loving me but hating the vessel that carries me.

22

I know by now that soulmates sound outdated and taboo, an overplayed trope that has become a cliche. But I still believe in a soulmate. Not in the "my other half, the one who can make me happy, the one who will turn my world into sunshine and rainbows" kind of way. More in the "home can be a human" kind of way. I do not want my soulmate to be my happiness, giving up far too much control. Instead, I want to be understood; to exist alongside another human being easily.

I am so tired of falling in love alone. But the only prevention tactic is to close yourself off from love, and I just cannot allow myself to fall into such hopelessness. I do not believe I am myself if I cannot love; if I cannot *fall* in love.

I will always speak—
Refusing to feel shame at exposing my affections.
I will tell you I love you
Even if I know you do not feel the same—
Even if I know an inevitable sorrow is soon to follow.
The simple thought of dying before expressing
Induces me through fear.
It is more pitiful, to me, to say too little
Than to say too much.

To the moon.

29

I have always found the moon quite loving. Every night, without question, she appears. Stalking down every turn and winding down any road, she is rather inescapable. The moon finds itself in a constant cycle of regrowth, incrementally revealing herself to the stars. The moon knows me better than any human ever will. I tell the moon my deepest secrets, and she hides them for me in her shadows until I am ready to revisit my turbulences the next night.

The inescapability of the moon–I think that is what draws me to her. There is no doubt when I step out each night, she will be there, and if I have failed to find a lover who will caress me through the night, I can stand underneath the easing moonlight and be touched by its warmth. For once, I am the one who chooses whether or not to return. I am usually the moon. The constant for others, waiting every night in hopes that they may settle for the glowing warmth I provide.

35

I never thought it was possible to fall in love alone before you. Unfortunately, it is.

Everyone tells you to be careful in relationships.

No one warns you of the consequences of falling in love alone—

No one warns you of the consequences of unrequited love.

Some part of my heart will always love you. You changed everything for me. I did not know what love was when I first started falling for you. In all fairness, I was quite young, but as my feelings grew, I did too. Maybe that is why I need to get all of this off my chest: because I grew up, became who I am, whilst falling harder and harder for you. I need to separate the two points in my life, and I hope this can be the beginning of that process.

Sometimes I wonder how much easier it would have been not falling for you but in a way, I needed to. Know that I will never regret loving you.

I know there is nothing to be done about the things I say. I hope you know that is not the point of this letter–for something to come of it. Rather, these letters serve more as a 'I gotta find some inner peace with my past' kind of thing. In the simplest terms I can think of, you remind me of the moon. When I catch a glimpse of you, it feels like that moment you see the month's full moon for the first time–it never gets old, it never gets less beautiful, and your soul feels content. Maybe you remind me of the moon because she really knows how I feel about you. She listened to me on every late night drive, and understood what it was I felt before even I realized. And now it kind of sucks because it has become impossible to look at the moon, and not think of you.

There have been so many points these past few months where I wanted to swipe up on your story, or tell you condolences, and I am sorry I was too scared to. I hope you know I will always be there for you, but I didn't want you to think I wasn't okay with letting you go. It's difficult for me to describe my feelings because I've felt them alone, for so long, that they're unlike anything I've ever experienced before. It's been you for so long that trying to move on from you is like trying to get over the ending of your favorite 17 season comfort show. My affection for you has been such a constant in my life that it only feels natural to love you.

I close my eyes as a memory of you blinks behind them
Blinding me from within.
But with each day that passes your face disintegrates;
The contours of your expression blurring.
You become what I fear most:
That soon, remembering the shallow dips of your smile
Or the curvature of your cheeks
Or the way your eyes felt looking into mine
Or the exact hew of the sun radiating from your golden skin
Will evade me.
That I will no longer remember the warmth I felt when you
looked at me.

The way we looked at each other
was enough for me
to find peace, because behind
your eyes I found proof of another
universe
where we are
together in this love.

42

Before,
When I caught a glimpse of you
Your soul would feel like everything good in this world.
I think if I saw you now
And really stared at you
I would just feel a sense of mourning
For that soul I so strongly and stupidly had faith in.

43

Last week, as I drove to the night's adventure in Brooklyn, I looked up at the moon. The glaring purity of its glow made me smile. Not until many hours later, while my mind dwindled itself down to sleep, did I realize...I looked up at the moon and did not think of you.

A love letter to my little friend.
While our physical time together may have been small,
Thinking of you will always create glowing moonlight
on the rose blushes of my cheeks.

I know these letters are the last things you need in life right now, the confessions of a smitten 18 year old. But to be honest, these letters are more for me than you. I know what that sounds like–and I'm sorry. I can't move on with my life until I am certain I will leave this earth having told those important to me exactly how I feel. I guess that is a bit dramatic, but I just need to know you've understood my feelings for you. These feelings may not be reciprocated in the same way – that is completely okay. I never expected them to be.

One day I will gain the wisdom to know not to fall in love with those I cannot have. But for now, here we are. In all honesty, I have always wondered how so many people can know you and not fall in love with you. My mind lacks that capability.

I once worried about what you'd make of all of this, but you know me well enough to know I am not that type of person - the type to obsess.

I may romanticize and feel emotions deeply, but that is nothing to be ashamed of. I have experienced so much in such a short time, and I am proud of myself for it. I am proud of my uninhibited being.

Your scent

Just reminiscing on it carries me back to you.

Alcohol and cigarettes.

Two vices forming my concept of you, my virtue.

Miscellaneously mixed with your innate softness,

Its lingering breathing out from the part in your lips.

Oh god - *your lips.*

Through their sweetness, feeling your vulnerability.

I long to experience it again.

Please, save what is left of it for me.

There I stood, soapy hands fumbling away at the long ignored clutter of dishes, feet firmly placed on the creaky chestnut wood of my first apartment, and it subtly hit me – the validity of what we had is not dependent on how he felt. What I felt was enough…it was enough to make it real. While I know he cared for me, his ceaseless maturity made it near impossible to see what he truly felt, if he possibly shared the same giddy, 18-year-old sense of complete infatuation. But I didn't need to see it. What I needed was evident in the way he reaffirmed my beauty when I failed to see it myself. In the way he could discern the discontented tone in which I spoke to myself, always sure to give me the comforting, "you are enough". Not those exact words, but in his own way he made certain I knew I was. In the way he chose to touch me, once the sexual sessions subsided and we sat contently outside, the hand that found its way to my knee. Within all his little ways, he made me fall in love, and that is all I need to know. I was granted the privilege of being cared for by him in a way that allowed me to love him.

52

I am unsure why I told you so much about those I loved before. I think it was more about the fact that they had loved me. I wanted you to know others had viewed me in such a way - others fell in love with me, craved me, needed me, *chose* me.

Maybe then you would too.

I still remember the hesitation in your words,
Too scared to share certain things.
While I remained patient, I laughed to myself.
Not at your shame
But at the belief that what you would say
could possibly make me think of you
as anything less than a masterpiece.

It's been awhile now.
Awhile since I rested with my ear to your chest,
Listening to your heart beat, pretending it was beating for me.
As if every ounce of blood intently pumped throughout your body
Was purposefully done for me,
To stay alive with me.
That would only be fair,
It was what my heart was doing in that moment -
continuing to beat for you.
My pulse yearning to be in synchronization with yours.
Even now, with the thousands of miles separating us
I still sometimes feel my heart reaching out for yours.
Urging itself out of my chest to go and find you.
Sad.
Isn't it?
Is it?
Without regard for well being,
Or the brain's better judgement,
This heart is willing to destroy me
just to love you.

55

The thing is, I do not think I could classify this as unrequited love. You must have some sense of how I adore you by this point, and that almost makes it harder. Knowing you slightly scratched the surface of my love, but hold no inclination toward diving in the deep end. So I remain here, peering up through the water at the blurry sunlight of your love, patiently waiting for you to reach in. Drowning.

I have an inkling you never will.

You entrance me.

Any day, any time, any reason -

I will answer you.

That is what terrifies me.

I belong to you,

and you didn't even ask me.

I love you,

and you don't even need me.

We both know that if you requested,

I would choose you, and come running.

And although I hate to admit it,

I wait for the day you ask me to love you.

The day you give purpose to this credulous devotion of mine.

You were my most precious melody,

but he sang for me.

I gave you every chance I possibly could,

You remained mute.

There is nobody to blame.

Twice.
Just twice,
And I am left with all of this.

The muse I long envisioned came alive in you.

I am unsure of how to let him go.

> How does one replace a muse?

> How does one let go of a muse they can no longer turn

> into art,

> that they know they should no longer write about?

And even more daunting,

What becomes of an artist with no muse?

There are millions of you out there,

and millions of me.

But us,

us is not something easily found again.

Even if you do not feel the way I do,

I find reconciliation in the mutually understood rarity

of our vulnerability with one another.

We were opposites

and yet exactly the same.

This bare minimum acknowledgment will have to do for now.

Why?

Why, why, *why.*

My life is everything I ever wanted,

Everything I ever wished for.

I should be happy.

I never imagined actually existing in this self.

So tell me why I felt more content

More full more satisfied

More satiated

Those nights I lived with nothing

except for you.

I wonder if you heard me,

That second night.

In between the muffles and moans,

So hesitantly quiet and alluded with fear,

Baby, I whisper.

Instead of the usual term of endearment.

It felt like the last time,

And I knew I would never forgive myself if we became platonic friends,

And I never had the chance to call you that.

I wonder if you heard me.

I am unsure if I hope you did

Or if I should pray that you did not.

La dernière fois

I have a French test tomorrow.

Tonight, as I studied, I came across the term in my textbook,

And I thought about our's.

Our dernière fois.

"Go all in."
That is what you said
About my new guy
Minutes after you said you liked me.
We both know what you meant.
We like each other, but please fall for someone else,
We can't.
And so now, I must.

Age.
I actually looked up the definition
and wondered what it would say,
What simple words it would dwindle the concept down into.
The duration of time something has been alive.
The length of existence.
Here lies the fatal flaw: living is not synonymous with existing.
We hear this all the time but
Now I understand why its repetition is so prevalent.
Sure, you have existed longer–
      So what?
It is a shame this fact stops us from living,
Stops us from loving.

How sad

How many stories like ours there must have been.

Left to wither throughout the abandoned corridors of history.

Love stories like ours.

The ones that were never given the chance to begin

From fear of outer perceptions.

The ones that started with THE END.

Oh god.

I want you.

I fear I always will.

You have confirmed now what I always hoped for
But never truly convinced myself of.
Actually, that is untrue.
I knew our connection was not a one sided affair, it takes two,
But outer influences made me feel like my initial inclinations were
juvenile and naive.
Either way,
I know now.
That you felt for me what I feel for you.
What I wasn't quite prepared for
Was the screeching reality that this changes nothing.
Except now I know that if we weren't so terrified, we could be
something.
I cannot tell which is more unbearable,
the knowing or the unknowing.

I once worried I was too much.

My desire for a life of splendor unrealistic.

Not monetarily, splendor in the form of

Art viewings at The Louvre,

Late nights of discussing said art

Listening to Jazz and eating good food in the city

Ecstasy lined nights in your arms.

A life overcome by culture, beauty, art,

Passion.

I once thought it was unrealistic,

But you made it real.

I had it,

I had someone who understood why I am incapable of settling

for a life of less.

Please, let us live this life together.

At this point, I might as well title this book your name.
4 consonants, 3 vowels.
I guess that is how I know you really are my muse;
My very own work of art to analyze and write on.
What a lucky reviewer I am.

Last night I wanted to scream at you through the phone
Grow some balls and love me
My initial reaction one of anger
Because I stand here ready to say *fuck it,*
Ready to *just love each other*
And you keep stopping me.
I can now look back with the temperance to recognize why you are
logical.
You are not just protecting yourself but protecting me.
And though I appreciate the sentiment
Just let me destroy myself in this passion.
      Although,
            I would not want to if our commitment brought
            with it your crucifixion.
                I understand.

I find peace in believing
In some other dimension
Circumstances gave us the chance to grow together—
Our love forming around one another.
And although it sounds skeptical,
It remains the only hope I have:
That in another world we are not damned
But were meant to be.

It is getting harder and harder to fall asleep.
I do not have the energy to dream of you
Knowing I will wake up without you near me.
I use the moon to comfort me, but tonight,
even she cannot heal me.
The sharp nightly smack needed for the window to lock
absorbs the remaining energy in my arm before
hesitantly
my eyelids give up the fight.
My body forcefully succumbs to the screeching silence
and lack of moonlight.

I thought of you today,

and it felt nostalgic.

A dreaded feeling

signaling that I can no longer view my love for you

or my formation of *us*

as a characteristic of my present life.

I have always held this overwhelming fear,

fear that I will lose connections with those I care for.

I am lucky enough to call you a friend,

but let me not pretend.

> Let me not pretend
>
> I do not envy the woman who receives the honor of
> loving you,
>
> Of being loved by you.
>
>> But I want you to have her.
>>
>> I want you to be happy.
>>
>>> You are a good man,
>>>
>>> One who deserves it.

75

I fell apart last night.

It was a mix of things,

but it would be dishonest to say you were not a factor.

More than anything, it was the emotional frustration I felt...

76

...I was crying for you,
And he was the one that held me through it.

To the man who taught me
I am, in fact, easy to love. Thank you.
Thank you, thank you, thank you.

You were the first person to make me feel as though you recognized my worth; that I was worthy of more than most were willing to give. I never expected it to make me feel the way it did, almost un-easing. Somehow your complete and utter faith in my worth, and in your desire to be with me, made me insecure. For the first time, someone wholeheartedly chose me, but it made me wonder *why*. I am still unsure of how to cope with the unwavering affection you give me, how to cope with someone *choosing* to love me.

I am unsure of where we will go. I wish I could say I know it is you, but for now, please find comfort in my appreciation for you. I love you, in the simplest way. In the most refined and pure form of the phrase.

I am certain that within you, salvation was formulated. And if I cannot mutually provide you with it, I hope you find the one who pays my atonement.

But I hate to focus on such circumstances. For now, I plan on loving you as long as I can; as long as my love for you brings justice to the term.

All I know
Is when I lay my head on your chest
Your heartbeat carries me to sleep.
My sweetest lullaby.

I used to think love was a fiery passion—
A few burns here and there the normal sacrifice.
Looking back at my blistering sores I realize
That type of love was my very own brand of hell.
You are my penance.

I heard it repeatedly.
"You deserve the best"
As if I did not know.
What I failed to be told,
And what you proclaimed to me,
You deserve the best *and I get to give it to you.*
What a difference.

To be in the present moment of us,
An *us* I can claim,
To be in the middle of a love this wholesome,
It feels unreal.

> Even though I knew
> Eventually
> I would find someone to love me,

>> The problem with an eventually
>> Is that it leaves room for disbelief;
>> for doubt.

The type of love that strips you,
Removing barricades of overly proclaimed
confidence and walls of forced strength.
And while this may feel like a weakening,
It is quite the opposite.
The type of love that cuts you down
So that you may grow again
But this time in an environment where
you do not have to defend yourself.
A love that lets you be re-planted
In soil which promises to nourish you.

Those first few days after we exchanged I love you's
my voice could not help itself.
I think I uttered those words to you over a million times.
You were the first person who let me proclaim it so proudly,
who found pride in my love for them,
and who responded with the same passion

You took my hand,

Pressing it to the pulsing of your chest.

"Do you hear that?", you asked.

I giggled in confusion.

> *Beat-beat*

> *Beat-beat*

Pressing my hand even closer,

Tapping the two fingers resting on it to the beating, you chanted -

> *Del-bar*

> *Del-bar*

I swear my own heart stopped.

It is now, as I sit here writing this, that I realize.

You made sure I knew.

You made sure I knew your heart was beating for me.

92

Not *The End,*
But a pause.

To the reader, now having read.

There is no dedication I can write that would be good enough; worthy of thanking you for every word you waded through. Asking you to read, I wanted to be sure I held nothing back. I wanted to be sure I placed my heart in your hands. I hope you feel as though I did. More than anything, I hope you can take part of my heart with you–keeping it tucked away for those nights you may need the added comfort.